★★★★★★★★★★★★★★★★★★★★★★★★★★

WAR HEROES OF AMERICA

Sam Houston
OF TEXAS

MATTHEW G. GRANT

Illustrated by Harold Henriksen

GALLERY OF GREAT AMERICANS SERIES

★★★★★★★★★★★★★★★★★★★★★★★★★★

Sam Houston

OF TEXAS

Text copyright © 1974 by Publication Associates. Illustrations copyright © 1974 by Creative Education. International copyrights reserved in all countries. No part of this book may be reproduced in any form without written permission from the publisher. Printed in the United States.

Library of Congress Number: 73-18080   ISBN: 0-87191-299-6

Published by Creative Education, Mankato, Minnesota 56001
Distributed by Childrens Press, 1224 West Van Buren Street, Chicago, Illinois 60607

Library of Congress Cataloging in Publication Data
Grant, Matthew G
  Sam Houston of Texas
  (His Gallery of great Americans series. War heroes of America)
  SUMMARY: An easy-to-read biography of the soldier and politician who helped gain Texas independence from Mexico and became first president of the new Republic of Texas in 1836.
  1. Houston, Samuel, 1793-1863 — Juvenile literature. (1. Houston, Samuel, 1793-1863. 2. Generals. 3. Texas — History) I. Henriksen, Harold, illus. II. Title.
F390.H84723   976.4'04'0924 (B) (92)   73-18080
ISBN 0-87191-299-6

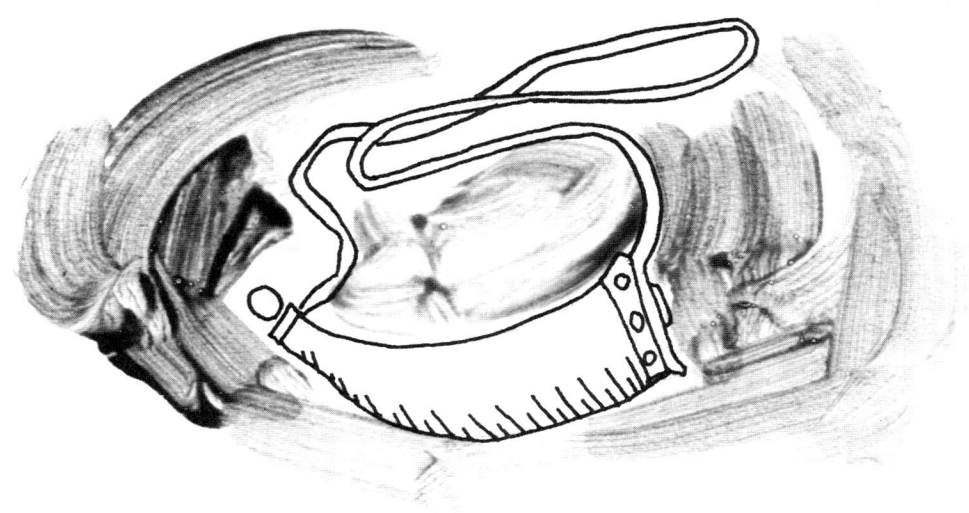

CONTENTS

WILDERNESS BOY	7
BIG MAN IN TENNESSEE	14
A GENERAL IN TEXAS	18
LONE STAR AND RAVEN	27

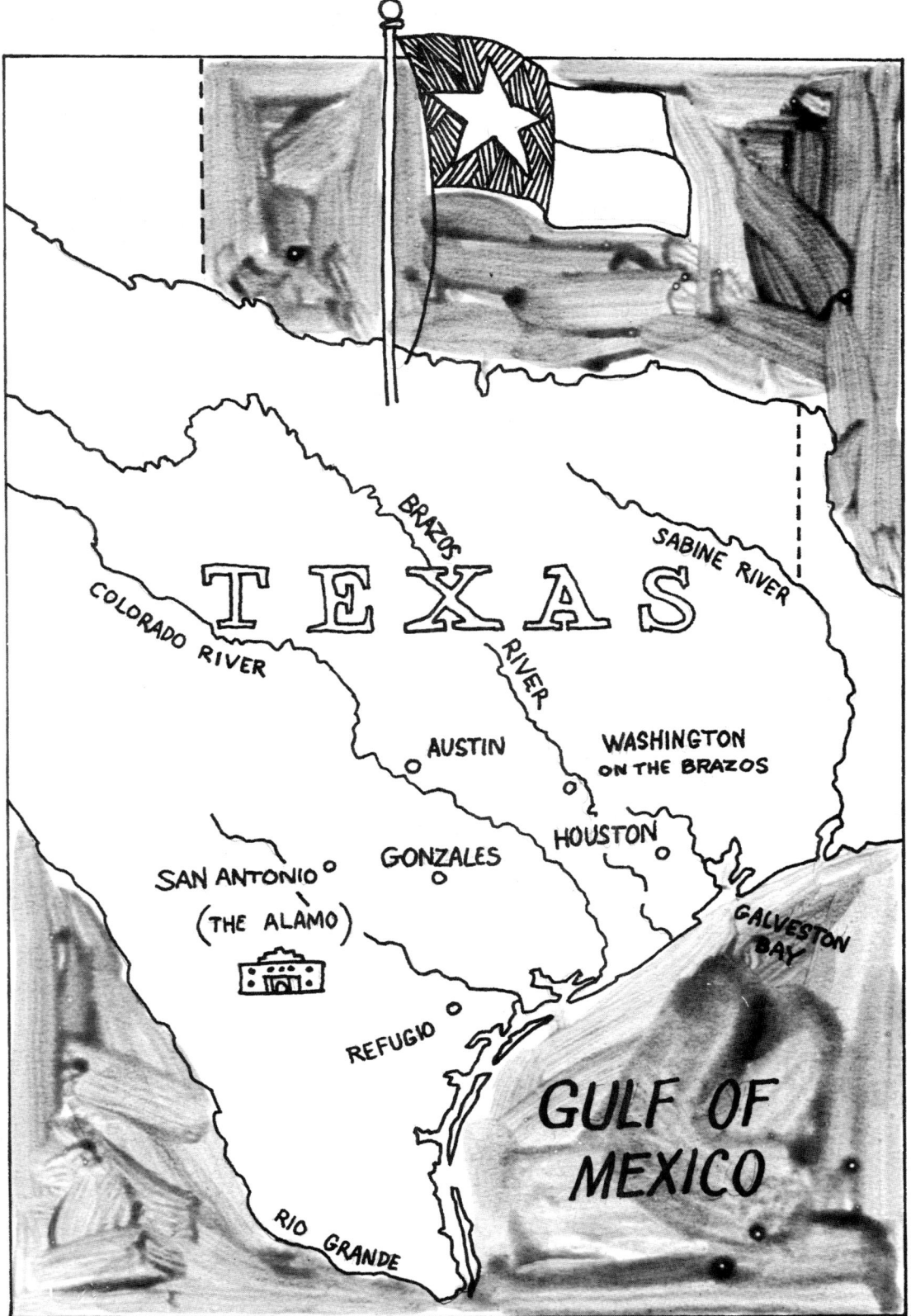

WILDERNESS BOY

Before he died, Major Sam Houston of Virginia said to his wife: "Take the children and go West." So in 1807, Widow Houston and her nine boys and girls went to the Tennessee wilderness.

Fourteen-year-old Sam was the fifth child. He helped his older brothers build the house and the farm buildings out of logs. He helped clear out brush and plant crops. It was hard, dull work and Sam hated it. He wished he could have been a soldier like his father. He spent long hours wandering in the woods. In winter, he read all the books he could find.

His family let him go to work for a storekeeper in nearby Maryville. But this work suited him no better than farming. He ran away and went to live with the Cherokee Indians along the Tennessee River. Chief Oo-loo-te-ka liked Sam and adopted him. He called the boy Co-lon-neh—The Raven.

Sam stayed with the Indians for nearly three years. It was the happiest time of his life.

When Sam was 19, he had to leave the Indians. He had bought many presents from the Maryville store for his red friends, and now he had to pay the bill.

He opened a school. Sam had had very little schooling himself. But he was very clever and had read many books. His tales of Indian life delighted the children and kept them from misbehaving. His school was a great success and soon his bills were paid.

It was the year 1812. War broke out between America and Britain. The British roused the Creek Indians in Alabama, who began to attack white settlers.

Sam joined the army of General Andrew Jackson. He became an officer. In 1814 he fought bravely at the battle of Horseshoe Bend, Alabama. As he led his men forward, he was hit by an arrow but told a soldier to pull it out.

BIG MAN IN TENNESSEE

War wounds put Sam out of action for some time. Andy Jackson found out about Sam's years with the Cherokee. He sent Sam to convince the tribe to move West. The Indians moved, and Sam received government thanks.

Sam liked being with important government men. He decided to become a lawyer, and enter politics himself. It was almost as easy for Sam to become a lawyer as a teacher. After studying for six months, he passed his exam. Because he was a friend of General Jackson, he was invited to run for district attorney. In 1823, he was elected to

Congress. In 1828, when Jackson became President, Sam Houston was Governor of Tennessee.

He was only 35, six feet two inches tall, handsome and clever. People talked about running him for President. He fell in love with Eliza Allen and married her the next year. But poor Eliza had not loved him. Her parents pushed her into the marriage and she was very unhappy with Sam. Finally, they separated. Ugly rumors began to fly and Sam's political career was ruined. He had to resign the governorship.

A GENERAL IN TEXAS

Sam went West, to the Indian Territory, where his old friends the Cherokees now lived. He stayed with Chief Oo-loo-te-ka. When the Indian agent made trouble, Sam went to Washington as a Cherokee "ambassador."

President Jackson promised to help the Cherokees. Then he gave Sam a new job. He was to go to Texas, which was then a part of Mexico. Many of the settlers there were Americans. Jackson had tried to buy Texas from Mexico and failed. But perhaps there was another way to acquire the territory!

Sam Houston went to find out. In 1833 he wrote to Jackson that Texas was ready to break away from Mexico.

Sam quickly plunged into Texas politics. He was elected to public office. Meanwhile, English-speaking Texans planned how to throw off Mexican rule. In 1835, war finally broke out.

Sam Houston was made a general in the Texas Army. He learned that the Mexican President, General Santa Anna, was coming north with a large army. By Spring, 1836, Santa Anna was at the Alamo.

A small force of Texans tried to hold the Alamo fort. At the same time, Texas statesmen were having a meeting, setting up a new government. Sam Houston signed Texas' Declaration of Independence on March 2, 1836. Then he set out with an army to save the Alamo. But he was too late. The Alamo fell on March 6 and all of its defenders were killed. The Texans shouted: "Remember the Alamo!"

At first, Sam Houston's army fled before the larger force of Santa Anna. Then Sam got

some badly needed cannons and went after the Mexicans. The two armies met near the San Jacinto River on April 21. The cannons of Texas fired broken horseshoes and the men of Texas charged, shouting: "Remember the Alamo!"

Sam Houston was wounded in the leg. His fighting Texans crushed the army of Santa Anna.

As Houston lay under a tree, his men brought him a prisoner dressed in civilian clothes. It was General Santa Anna. Not only the battle, but the entire Texas war for independence was won.

When Texans held their first election in fall, Sam Houston was chosen to be president. One of his first acts was the freeing of Santa Anna. Mexico finally recognized the Republic of Texas.

LONE STAR AND RAVEN

Houston wanted Texas to become one of the United States. This finally happened in 1845. Meanwhile, Sam married Margaret Lea and the couple had a son. Sam had a happy home life at last.

In 1846, he was elected U. S. Senator from Texas. He served the people of the Lone Star State in this office until 1859. It was a time when the issue of slavery began dividing the United States. Sam, who had fought so hard for union, could not bear to see Texas drift into the ranks of the slave states, with their talk of secession. But most people in Texas were in favor of slavery. Sam was a maverick.

He ran for governor, with the promise that he would keep Texas in the Union, and he won. But he could not stop his state from seceding in 1861. He refused to take an oath supporting the Confederate States of America. He said: "I love Texas too much to bring strife and bloodshed upon her."

Sam Houston was removed from the governorship and the Civil War began.

He was 68 years old and very tired. His beloved son, Sam, Jr., became a Confederate soldier. He was wounded at Shiloh, then sent home to his parents. As the South began to lose the war, Sam made plans for rebuilding Texas as a republic. But twilight was falling for the old Raven. He died in Huntsville on July 26, 1863, calling out the names of those he loved most—his wife Margaret and his state, Texas.

GALLERY OF GREAT AMERICANS SERIES

INDIANS OF AMERICA
- GERONIMO
- CRAZY HORSE
- CHIEF JOSEPH
- PONTIAC
- SQUANTO
- OSCEOLA

EXPLORERS OF AMERICA
- COLUMBUS
- LEIF ERICSON
- DeSOTO
- LEWIS AND CLARK
- CHAMPLAIN
- CORONADO

FRONTIERSMEN OF AMERICA
- DANIEL BOONE
- BUFFALO BILL
- JIM BRIDGER
- FRANCIS MARION
- DAVY CROCKETT
- KIT CARSON

WAR HEROES OF AMERICA
- JOHN PAUL JONES
- PAUL REVERE
- ROBERT E. LEE
- ULYSSES S. GRANT
- SAM HOUSTON
- LAFAYETTE

WOMEN OF AMERICA
- CLARA BARTON
- JANE ADDAMS
- ELIZABETH BLACKWELL
- HARRIET TUBMAN
- SUSAN B. ANTHONY
- DOLLEY MADISON